GREATER ESTIMATIONS

Bruce Goldstone

About how many times do I bark in one day?

About how long can I stand up like this?

About how fast can I run away from all these dogs?

Henry Holt and Company
New York

To Eleanor, who is 6—
I estimate she knows about 7,000 words in English
and just as many in German.

Thanks for the bears (and some other stuff) to Anne Barry; Marion Boultbee; Cooper,
Campbell, Dossie, and Wyatt Boynton; Sydney Dooley; Sam, Lucy, and Jack Fell; Ann,
Stona, Amelia, and Claire Fitch; Ed Goldman; Lea Guertin; Aisling Hegarty; Ariel Iasevoli;
Ann Kaplan; Sydney McCort; Kan Nagata; Robb Riedel; Katherine Sharpe; Stephanie Sim.
Thanks also to John Sabatini for his artful help, Nick Falletta for his good advice,
and Bobby Kelly for being a good pal.

Henry Holt and Company, LLC, *Publishers since 1866*
175 Fifth Avenue, New York, New York 10010
www.HenryHoltKids.com

Henry Holt® is a registered trademark of Henry Holt and Company, LLC.
Copyright © 2008 by Bruce Goldstone
Photo credits: All images © Arnold and David Katz/Bruce Goldstone with the following exceptions: pp. 10 and 11,
© Wendy Smith; pp. 12 and 13, © PhotoLiz; p. 17, © Image Source; p. 19, © Achim Prill; p. 24, © Ivan Cholakov
(jet), © Andreas Meyer (giraffe), © MaxFX (wind turbine), © Christine Balderas (palm tree), © Joyce Sherwin
(totem pole), © Jill Lang (Cape Hatteras Lighthouse), © Kenneth C. Zirkel (school bus), © Tomasz Pietryszek
(truck), © Lior Filshteiner (kite), © Michael Ledray (girl flying kite), © Helen Shorey (Tower of Pisa), © Akrytova
Tetiana (Statue of Liberty), © Michael Zysman (skywriting plane), © Dainis Derics (blimp); p. 25, all images
© Eric Isselée with the exceptions of those © ANP, CP Photo, Phil Date, Fred Goldstein, Lijuan Guo,
Peter Hansen, John Holst, Vadim Kozlovsky, Erik Lam, Steve Mann, Robynrg, Chin Kit Sen, Roy Somech,
Ferenc Szelepcsenyi; p. 29, © Denis O'Regan/CORBIS; p. 30, © Lars Christensen; p. 31 (top), © Rick Seeney.
All rights reserved.
Distributed in Canada by H. B. Fenn and Company Ltd.

Library of Congress Cataloging-in-Publication Data
Goldstone, Bruce.
Greater estimations / Bruce Goldstone.
p.   cm.
ISBN-13: 978-0-8050-8315-6 / ISBN-10: 0-8050-8315-4
1. Estimation theory—Juvenile literature. I. Title.
QA276.8.G65 2008   519.5'44—dc22   2007040894

First Edition—2008 / Designed by Laurent Linn
Printed in the United States of America on acid-free paper. ∞

1 3 5 7 9 10 8 6 4 2

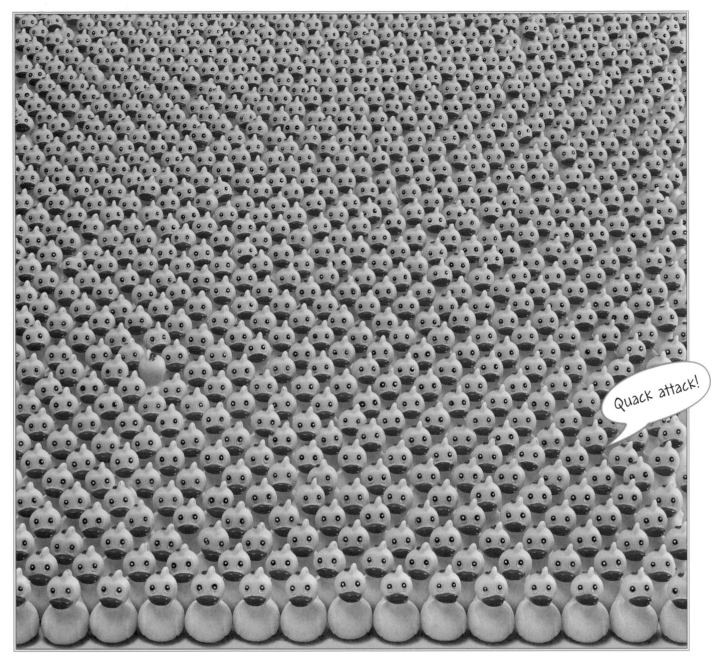

The ducks are coming! About how many rubber ducks are marching toward you?

Counting every duck could give you a headache. When you want to get a reasonable idea of how many things there are, try estimating.

An estimate is a good guess. When you estimate, you don't just pick a number out of the air—47 or 3,000 or 29 million. You take time to think about how big the number probably is. Eye training, clump counting, and box and count are three strategies that can help you come up with really great estimations.

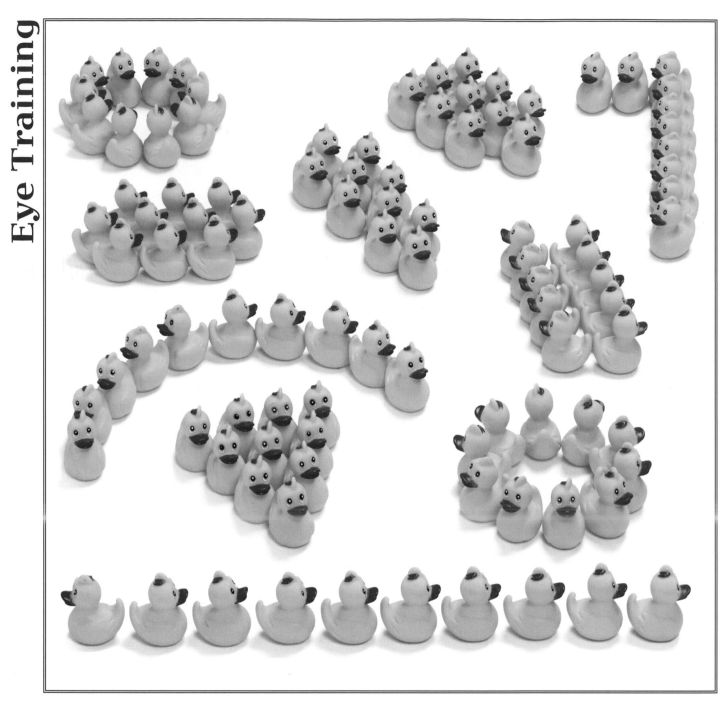

Train yourself to recognize groups of 10. What do 10 rubber ducks look like?

Hints Each group on this page has 10 ducks in it. Notice that groups of 10 things can have many different shapes.

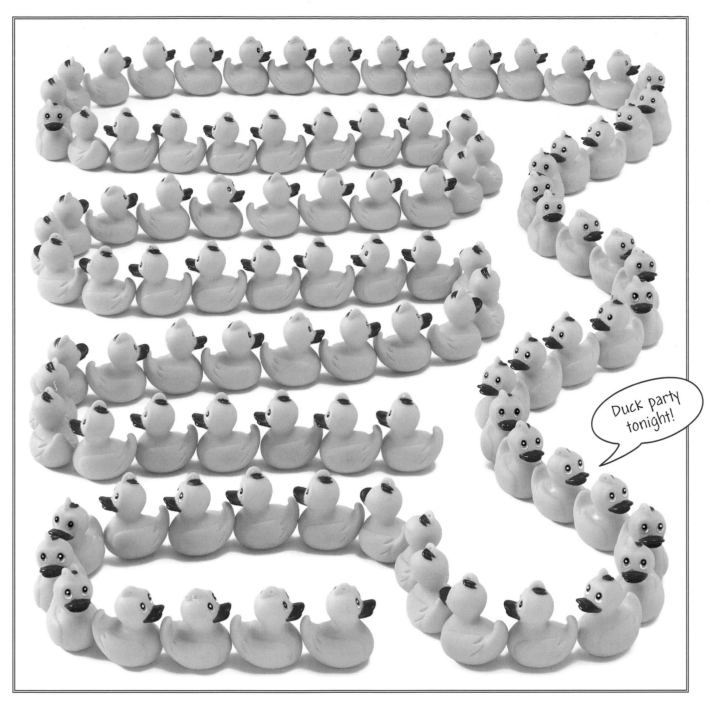

Duck party tonight!

What do 100 rubber ducks look like?

Hints: Want to see another group of 100 ducks? Just look over at page 4. There are 10 groups of 10 ducks— or 100 ducks in all.

What do 1,000 rubber ducks look like?

What do 10,000 rubber ducks look like?

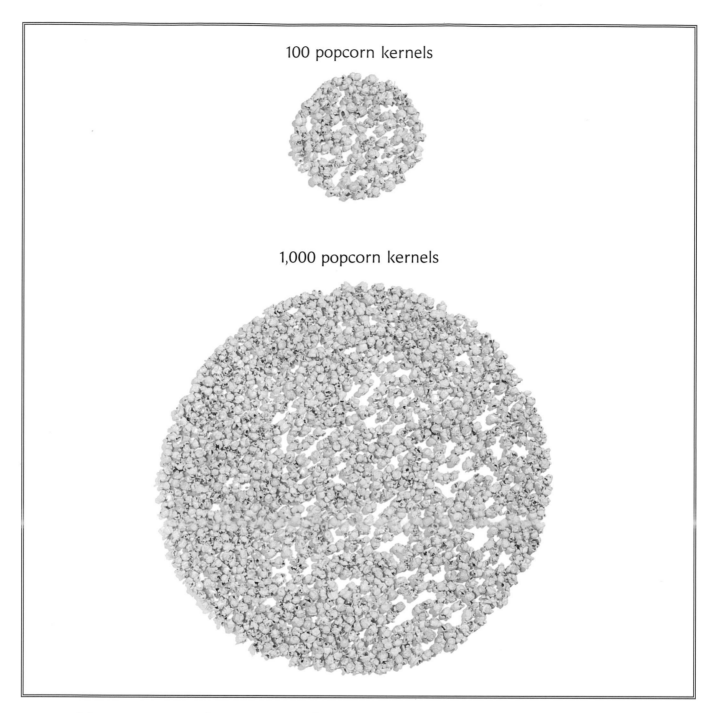

100 popcorn kernels

1,000 popcorn kernels

Looking at counted groups can help you estimate. Compare these groups of popcorn kernels. What do 100 kernels look like? What about 1,000?

**About how many kernels are in a giant tub
of movie popcorn?**

Hints: Use the counted groups of 100 and 1,000 kernels on page 8 as *benchmarks*. A benchmark is something you use to judge other things. By comparing the movie tub to the benchmarks, you can see that there are more than 1,000 kernels. Are there more than 2,000?

About how many skydivers do you see?

Clump counting is another useful estimation strategy. It helps you when objects are not evenly spread out across the picture.

Notice that the skydivers have formed a pattern. Look at this group of white skydivers. About how many divers are in it? Choose a nice round number and you can skip count. Skip counting is counting by twos, fives, tens, or other numbers.

You might estimate that there are about 50 divers in this clump. So skip count by 50s as you count each clump of divers: 50, 100, 150, 200, and so on. You will get to 500.

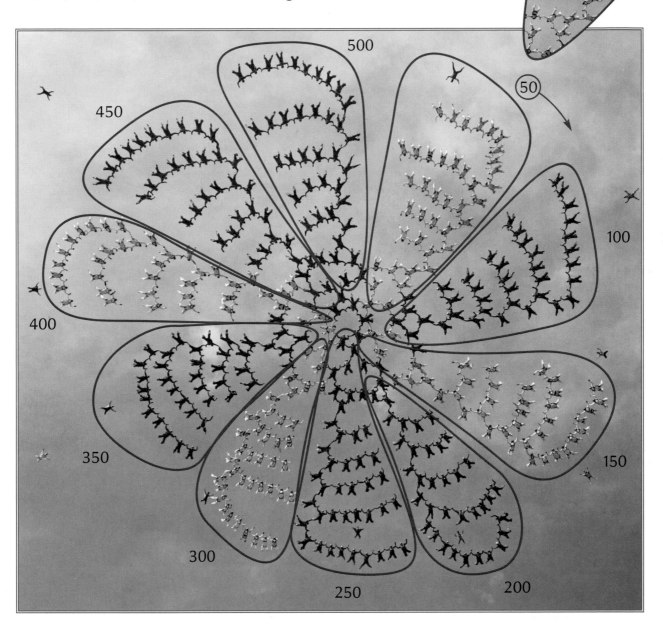

After you're done skip counting, you can adjust your estimate. There are actually fewer than 50 divers in each clump, so make your estimate somewhat lower than 500. You might decide on a final estimate of about 400 skydivers.

Two bees or not two bees?

About how many bees are buzzing in this photo?

Box and count is another estimation strategy. It's very useful when there are a lot of things that are evenly spread out, like the bees in this hive.

First, imagine dividing the picture into 100 small boxes. The grid on the next page shows what that looks like.

Then count the bees in a single box. Choose a box with an average number of bees.

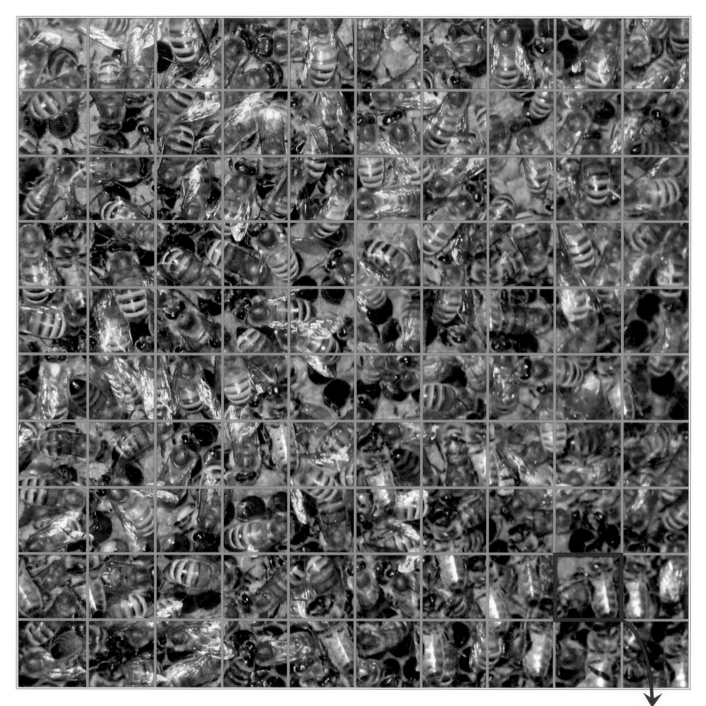

Look carefully to find the bees. Make sure you count bees, and not the honeycomb behind them. You might count 2 bees in this box. Even though some of each bee is cut off, you can use this count to get a reasonable estimate.

Multiply that number by 100 boxes to get your estimate. All you need to do is add two zeroes to the end of the number. If you estimated 2 bees in the little box, multiplying by 100 gives you an estimate of 200 bees.

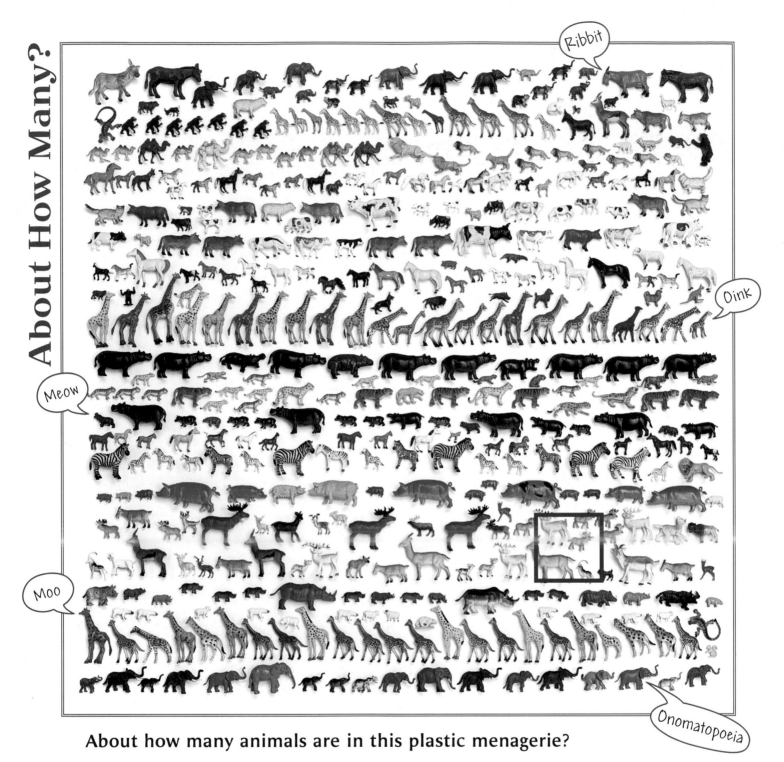

About how many animals are in this plastic menagerie?

Now you can practice using your estimation strategies. You might look back at the rubber duck benchmarks. Or you could count clumps of 10 animals. Use the $\frac{1}{100}$ box if you want to box and count.

Hints: Look at the ducks on pages 5 and 6. When you compare the 100 ducks with these animals, it is clear that there are more than 100 animals. Now compare the 1,000 ducks with these animals. What do you think: more ducks or more animals?

If you decide to box and count, use the red box to help. Count the animals inside and then multiply by 100. Remember, you just need to add two zeroes to your number.

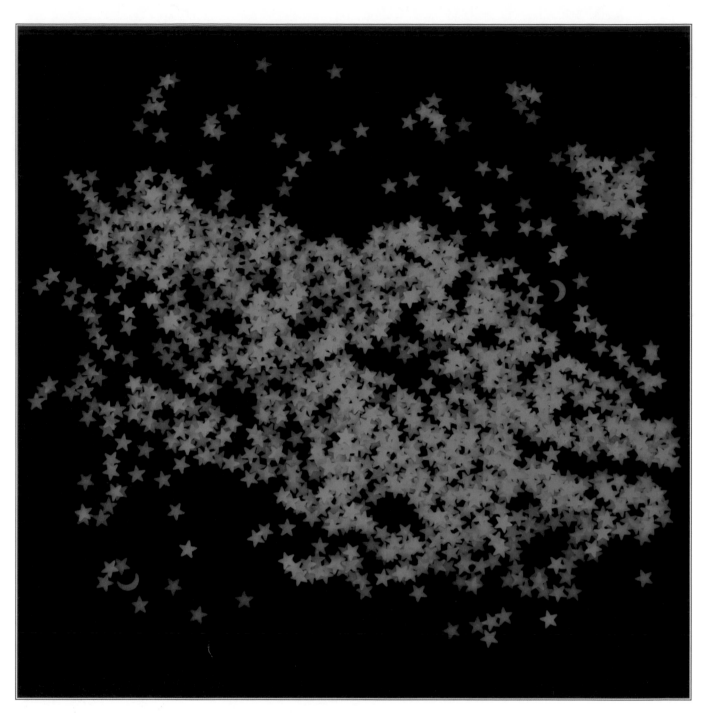

About how many glow-in-the-dark stars are shining?

Hints Clump counting could help you—try starting with a group of about 25 stars. But look closely and you'll find another clue. Some of the stars are stacked in piles of two, three, or four stars. You can see that the stars are brighter where more stars are stacked up. First use clump counting to estimate the top layer. Then add on to your estimate to account for the stars underneath.

About how many candies fill this photo?

Hints: You could clump count by types of candy, but notice that some of the candies are very large and others are very small. Choose a medium-size candy and estimate how many are there. Then use that number to clump count. If you box and count, choose a box that has a mixture of sizes. For example, you might count about 11 candies in the box shown.

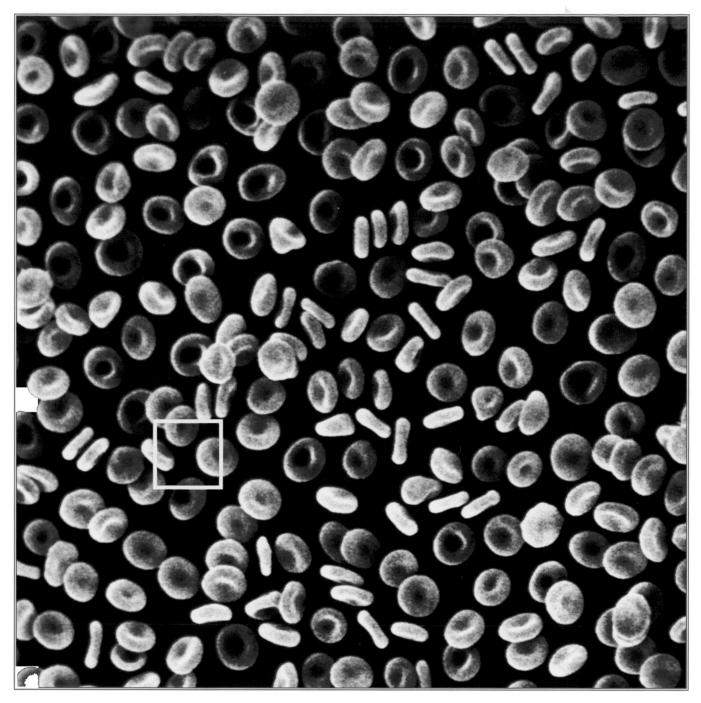

About how many red blood cells do you see?

This photograph of human blood was taken using a very powerful microscope. It shows red blood cells, which carry oxygen through the body. A single drop of blood contains about 5 million red blood cells!

Hints: This picture offers a perfect chance to box and count. The red blood cells are evenly spread out. About how many do you see in the box? How will you turn that number into a great estimation?

About how many flies make up this web? About how many spiders are waiting to catch them?

Hints: Try clump counting to estimate the number of flies. Look for groups of 10. The spiders are harder to see because they are in a big pile. Compare them with the ducks and the popcorn. Do you think there are 100 spiders? 1,000? 10,000?

18 About How Many?

About how many seeds do you set flying when you blow a dandelion?

Hints
You might estimate how many seeds are already flying off. Then use clump counting to imagine how many more groups the same size are still on the dandelion. Or you can use your eye training and decide if the total number of seeds looks to be closer to 100 or 1,000.

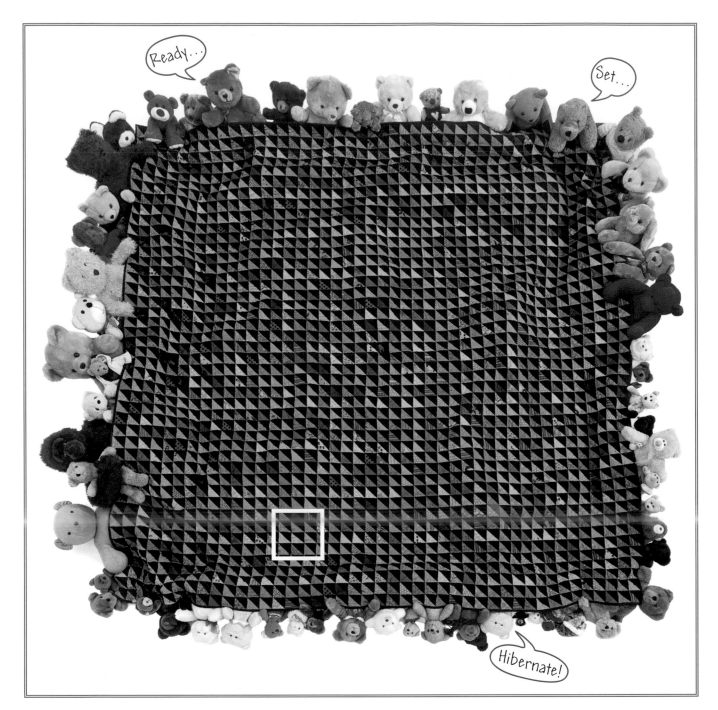

About how many teddy bears are tucked in for bed? About how many triangles are sewn together to make their quilt? About how many of the triangles are green? About how many are pink?

Hints: Count 10 bears and then clump count to estimate. The box shows about $\frac{1}{100}$ of the quilt. Count the triangles inside and then multiply by 100. Once you have estimated the total number of triangles, use that amount as the basis for estimating how many pink and green triangles there are. Do you think half of the triangles are green? What about pink?

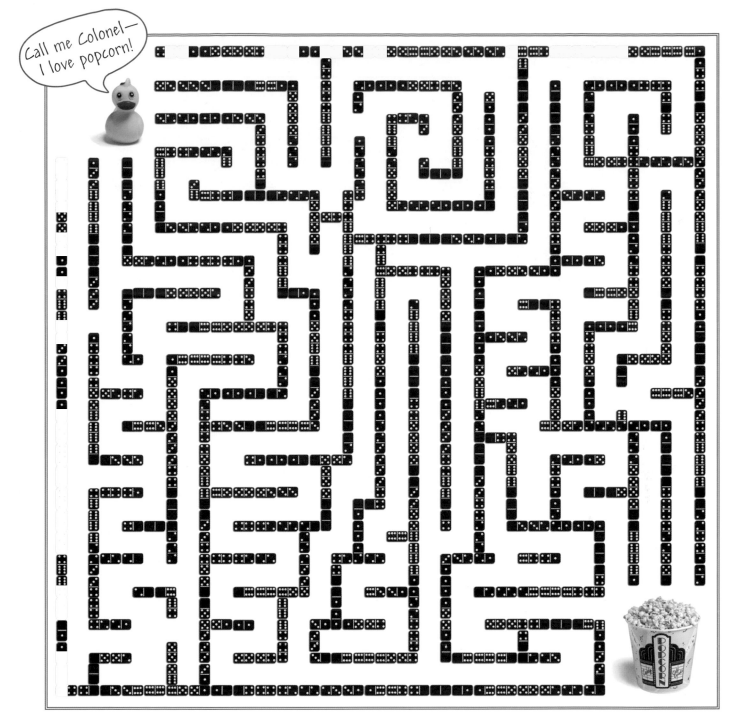

Call me Colonel—I love popcorn!

About how many dominoes are in this maze? About how many dots do you see? About how long will it take you to find a path from the duck to the popcorn?

About 1 inch

About 1 centimeter

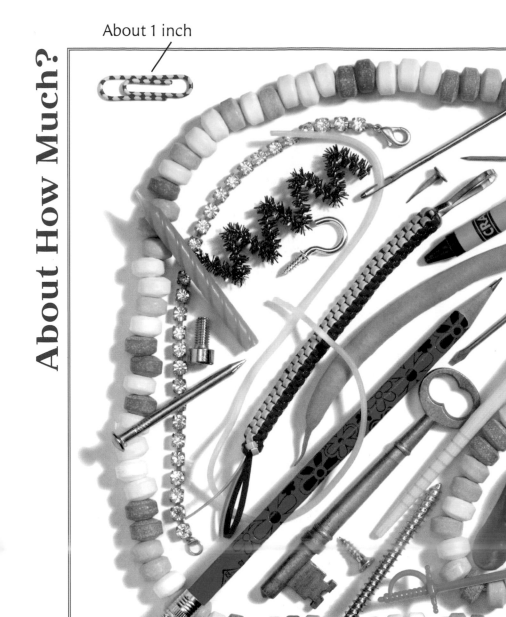

About how long are the things you see here?

You can estimate *how much* of something there is, instead of how many there are. You might want to estimate length. You can estimate length in inches. The paper clip is about one inch long. Use that number as a benchmark. About many paper clips long is the pencil? What about the candy necklace?

If you use the metric system, you can estimate length in centimeters. The mint is about one centimeter long. How many mints long is the gummy worm?

Hints: Two things can have about the same length, so your estimates can be the same. You might estimate that both the plastic sword and the needle are about 3 inches long. Your estimates can also include fractions. You might estimate that the small screw near the key is about $\frac{1}{2}$ inch long.

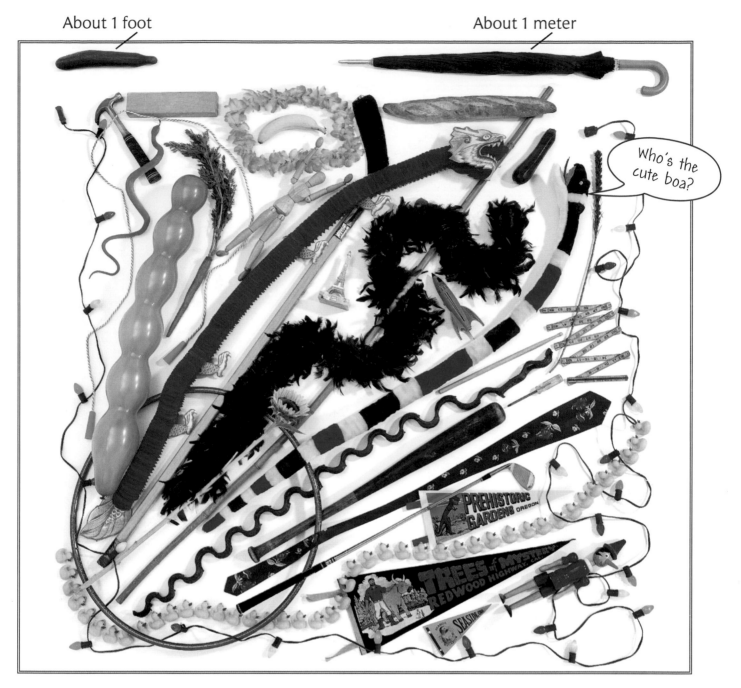

About 1 foot

About 1 meter

Who's the cute boa?

About how long is a baseball bat? A banana? A Hula Hoop?

You can estimate the length of larger things in feet. The cucumber is about one foot long. If you line up cucumbers, how many would you need to make a line as long as the baseball bat? The hockey stick?

In the metric system, you can estimate length in meters. The umbrella is about one meter long.

Hints Try to make your estimates consistent. That means they should make sense together. If you think the feather boa looks longer than the hockey stick, make sure your estimate for the boa is greater. One way to get consistent estimates is to begin with the object that looks shortest. Estimate its length. Then look for the next-shortest thing and estimate. Your estimate will either be the same or a little bit greater. Keep going, estimating things from shortest to longest.

About
100
feet

About
10
meters

About how tall is the palm tree? The Statue of Liberty?

You can estimate the height and length of very large objects, too. A jumbo jet is about 100 feet long. A school bus is about 10 meters long. Use these numbers as benchmarks to help you estimate the height or length of the other things on the page.

Hints

These estimates are like clump counting. Use the length of the jet as your clump of 100 feet. Skip count by hundreds to measure the taller things.

About 10 pounds   About 100 pounds   About 10 kilograms

Don't forget us fleas!

About how heavy is each dog?

You can estimate weight in pounds. The little Brussels griffon dog in the upper left corner weighs about 10 pounds. The Bernese mountain dog next to it weighs about 100 pounds. Use those benchmarks to help you estimate how much the other dogs weigh.

In the metric system, you can use kilograms to weigh how heavy something is. The pug in the upper right corner weighs about 10 kilograms.

Hints: To think about weight, imagine picking up each dog—or at least trying to! Some hands-on experience will help you get better at estimating weight. If you can find a willing dog, try this trick: Weigh yourself on a scale. Then hold the dog and weigh yourself again. The difference between the two weights is the weight of the dog.

If you don't have any dogs around, picking up other things can help you think about weight and size. Stop in the pet food aisle at a grocery store. Pick up a 1-pound box of biscuits. Then pick up a 5- or 10-pound bag of food. You can try larger bags, too.

About how big is a CD? A dime? A packet of ketchup?

You can use square inches to estimate the area of flat things, like a cracker or a leaf. Area is how much space something covers. The cheese cracker is about one square inch. About how many cheese crackers would you need to cover the baseball card? What about the bandage? You could cover the coins, too, though you'll have to imagine breaking the cheese cracker apart.

You can also measure area in square centimeters. The crunchy cereal is about one square centimeter. How many cereal squares would you need to cover the craft stick?

Hints

Remember, estimates don't have to be exact. If one coin is just a tiny bit larger than another one, it's okay to estimate that they're both about the same size.

About 1 ounce   About 10 ounces   About 50 milliliters

About how much liquid does each container hold? How much space is left over?

You can use ounces to measure how much something can hold. Look at the glasses that contain about one ounce and about 10 ounces. Use these pictures to help you estimate how much liquid is in the other glasses and containers.

You can also use milliliters to measure how much something holds. The glass in the upper right corner has about 50 milliliters of liquid in it.

Hints

You can train yourself to recognize ounces. Try this quick practice: Use a kitchen measuring cup to pour yourself one ounce of water and drink it. Then drink 10 ounces of water. You'll probably notice a big difference.

About how many people went to this concert in front of a castle?

Pictures taken from high overhead are called aerial photographs. They can be very helpful when you want to know how big a crowd is.

You can use clump counting even when the clumps are huge. There are about 10,000 people in the red clump. About how many of these clumps make up the crowd?

Hints

Skip counting with a number as big as 10,000 may sound complicated, but it's as easy as skip counting by tens. Just say "10 thousand, 20 thousand, 30 thousand," and so on.

Spring

Summer

About how many leaves are on this tree?

You can use the springtime picture to help you estimate how many leaves are on the tree in summer. It also helps to think about how trees grow. Leaves grow on twigs, which grow on branches. Each large branch grows out from the tree trunk.

Multiplication and a calculator can help, too. Try these steps.

• First, look at the big picture of one large branch. Estimate how many twigs you see.

• Next, estimate how many leaves grow on each twig.

• Use a calculator to multiply your two estimates together:
  (twigs on one branch) x *(leaves on one twig)* = *(leaves on one branch)*

• Finally, estimate how many large branches there are on this tree and multiply your estimate by that number:
  (leaves on one branch) x *(number of branches)* = *(leaves on tree)*

About how many hairs does a cat have?

No one has the time or patience to count all of the hairs on a cat. (And the cat probably wouldn't like it either!)

Sometimes doing a little research can help you make a great estimation. You need some facts to estimate how many hairs there are on a cat. Luckily, veterinarians know a lot about cats and their hair. They know these facts:

- An average cat has about 500 square inches of skin.
- A cat's hairs are closer together on its belly than on its back. On average, cats have about 60,000 hairs per square inch.*

You can put those facts together to estimate how many hairs a cat has. Multiply 500 by 60,000. Your calculator will tell you that a cat has more than 30 million hairs!

I know the answer. Ask me! Ask me!

*This sounds like a lot until you learn about the sea otter. It has the closest hairs of any animal—up to one million hairs per square inch!

About how many blades of grass are there on a football field?

The duck is sitting in one square foot of grass. Box and count to estimate blades of grass per square foot. Since there's more grass beneath what you see, you might estimate 40 blades of grass in the red box, which means about 4,000 blades of grass per square foot.

There are 48,000 square feet on a football field.* So multiply 48,000 by your estimate: 48,000 x 4,000 = 192,000,000.

You can round up to estimate that there are about 200 million blades of grass on a football field. That's a really, really big number—but don't stop there. Look around you and you'll find lots of other things to estimate every day—grapes in a bunch, letters on a sign, poppy seeds on a bagel, cans in a supermarket, snowflakes in a storm, sand at the beach. The possibilities are countless!

*A football field is 100 yards long and $53\frac{1}{3}$ yards wide. That's the same as 300 feet by 160 feet. Multiply those numbers together to find how many square feet in all.

A Note from the Author

I really do spend time wondering how many noodles there are in my bowl of soup. Or how many hairs I just brushed out of my dog. Or how many steps I'll take before I get to the next corner. I think estimating is a fun way to enjoy numbers.

But estimating is also a helpful tool that people use every day, on the job and at home. Doctors might need to estimate how many red blood cells a patient has. They can look at a sample like the photo on page 17. Astronomers can't count every star in the universe. They use brightness as one way to estimate how many stars are in a region—just like you used brightness to estimate glow-in-the-dark stars on page 15. Writers might estimate how many words they've written—or how many they have left to write.

Carpenters estimate lengths when they decide how much wood they need for a project. Designers of roller coasters estimate people's weights to make sure their rides will be safe. Cooks often estimate volume when they prepare foods, from fish sticks to cupcakes. You estimate area when you cut off a piece of wrapping paper, making sure it's big enough to cover your gift.

To prepare for events like parades and concerts, planners need to estimate about how many people will be there. At events like protest marches, estimating takes on a political edge. Different sides may have different estimates. People who participate in an event tend to overestimate how many people are there. Carefully analyzing aerial photographs produces more accurate numbers.

Estimating can lead to important conclusions. Scientists use photographs to estimate changes in the environment, like decreasing rain forests and shrinking glaciers. These estimates can help us understand what is happening and make accurate predictions about what will happen next.

Whether you're using numbers to solve real problems or just to have fun, one of the first steps is being comfortable with them. Practice with estimating can help you get used to numbers big and small. Scientists estimate that your brain has more than 100 billion nerve cells called neurons (that's 100,000,000,000). These cells send messages when you use your senses, feel emotions, or think about something. About how many of your neurons do you think go to work when you start estimating?

Cheers,

Bruce Goldstone